WALKS AROUND Castleton

10 WALKS UNDER 6 MILES

DALESMAN

Dalesman Publishing Company Ltd
Stable Courtyard, Broughton Hall,
Skipton, North Yorkshire BD23 3AE

First Edition 1998

Text © John Gillham

Illustrations © Christine Isherwood:
p4 redstart; p6 hart's tongue fern; p10 mountain pansies; p20 golden
plovers; p22 heather and bell heather; p30 mountain hare.

Cover: Cavedale by John Cleare

A British Library Cataloguing in Publication record
is available for this book

ISBN 1 85568 146 3

Printed by Amadeus Press, Huddersfield

Contents

Introduction

Historic Castleton sits snugly in the Hope Valley, guarded both by the shaly slopes of Mam Tor, the Shivering Mountain, and the square-towered Norman keep of Peveril Castle, which overlooks the village from a lofty limestone perch. On the far side of the valley, the green fields ascend from the cottages and the river, their hedges and walls arcing to accentuate the graceful slopes of the Great Ridge.

In the summer and on most weekends Castleton buzzes with tourists who come to sample a wide choice of cafes, shops, inns and B&Bs and to explore the many showcaves and walk the surrounding hills. For walking in the Peak National Park, it is unsurpassed.

In this book I have catered for the less experienced walker, who may not at first have the confidence or knowledge to tackle the big hills or vast peat moors such as Kinder Scout. The walks I have included should present no difficulties for these inexperienced walkers during the summer months when the paths should have dried out and be free from ice.

Walkers should make sure that all in their parties are wearing suitable boots, trainers or stout shoes with a good gripping sole, especially on routes to the higher ground – waterproofs will be necessary on unsettled days.

In spring and autumn there may be an added squelch to the walk caused by increased rainfall and that beloved creature, the cow, who delights in tramping in the wettest ground near to farm gates and stiles. At such a time boots are essential.

Many of the walks are in the Hope Valley, starting from either Castleton or neighbouring Hope. A few start a little further afield near Hathersage and the Derwent Valley reservoirs. All the walks are covered by the Ordnance Survey Outdoor Leisure Map 1: The Peak District – Dark Peak Area. These superb maps show the field boundaries and meticulous detail to help you stay on the path.

Cavedale and Winnats

A circular walk through two limestone ravines, and across a lofty
pastured plateau.
Length of walk: 5 miles.
Start/finish: Main car park, Castleton village centre.
Terrain: Fairly easy walking on well-marked paths and farm tracks.
The limestone rocks get a little slippery after rain.

From the car park turn left down Castleton's main street, then right along
Castle Street, passing the 12th century Norman church of St Edmund and
the youth hostel before veering left past the Market Place. At Bar Gate a
signpost points the way between cottages to the narrow neck of Cavedale,
where crags plummet down to the backyards of the stone-built cottages.
After squeezing between the rocks and through a gate, the path enters the
secretive limestone ravine. Now stony, the path climbs between ivory crags
that tower above lush, grassy slopes. Take care after rain, as the limestone
surface rocks have been weather-smoothed and can be very slippery.

On the right, the ruined keep of Peveril Castle looks down on the scene.
William Peveril, who was possibly the illegitimate son of William the
Conqueror, had the castle built not long after the Norman Conquest. The
keep was added in the 12th century by Henry II, a frequent visitor to these
parts. The castle was to change hands frequently in the Middle Ages. Its
owners included Eleanor of Castile, Simon DeMontfort and John of Gaunt.

As the path climbs, the valley becomes more shallow. After going over a
stile in the drystone wall on the right, follow the well-defined track that
continues across lofty fields. It passes through a gate in another wall before
being joined by a path that has descended the grassy hillside on the right.
The track divides soon after the junction. Take the left fork, which climbs
uphill, slightly away from the wall on the right. It meets the more circuitous
right fork at the top corner of the field. Go through the gate here and follow
a short stretch of walled track to a crossroads of routes. Turn right beyond
the gate here along a stony lane bound by drystone walls.

Where the lane turns right, leave it for a track that maintains direction
beyond a gate. The new track, one of those pleasing stony lanes with a grass

island through the middle, traverses a lofty plateau scattered with the workings of old lead mines. As the track nears the top of the hill, a stile on the right marks the point at which it should be abandoned for a trek across fields. A drystone wall on the left makes a foolproof guide to the top of the hill. Here, the whole of the Great Ridge is before your eyes; from the green whaleback of Rushup Edge, through Mam Tor, where there is an ancient fort, to Lose Hill, where it finally plummets to the fields of the Noe Valley.

From the top, a wide, grassy path descends among sparse outcrops and boulders of limestone. The path slowly curves right to the far corner of the high field, where it meets a track from Rowter Farm, a drystone wall and the B-road. To the left stands Oxlow House, a lofty, windswept farm.

The path resumes across the road beyond a stile. It passes the disused quarry on Windy Knoll. There's a cave worth exploring hereabouts. The bones of a grizzly bear, reindeer, bison and reindeer have all been found here and are said to date back to the last Ice Age. Just before reaching the A-road, turn right along a wide grassy path that aims for the farmhouse at Winnats Head. The path crosses the B-road encountered earlier and continues left of the farmhouse before joining the Winnats road.

The Winnats road, which plunges between limestone crags into the Hope Valley with a 1 in 5 gradient, has a long history. It began life as a jaggers' track where packhorse trains would cross the Pennines to convey salt from Cheshire and woollen goods from Yorkshire. In 1758 it became a turnpike road. Its new status was short-lived however, for the Manchester and Sheffield Turnpike Company built the ill-fated Mam Tor road to replace it (see walk 3 for the subsequent history).

It is not necessary to walk on the tarmac through Winnats, for a good path descends the grassy slopes beneath the crags on the left all the way to Speedwell Cavern, which started out life as a lead mine. The miners excavated a level through which they built a subterranean canal 500 yards long. Just beyond the canal is the Bottomless Pit, said to be so since the excavation material thrown in seemed to make no impression on its depth. Unfortunately, the uncommercial mine was forced to close. However, it

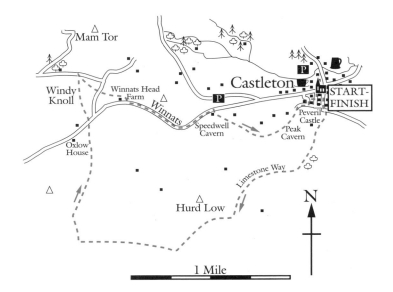

turned itself into a tourist attraction, and, if you fancy a boat trip with a difference, visitors are transported along the subterranean canal to a landing stage just short of the Bottomless Pit.

Just beyond the cavern building a path on the far side of the road takes the route through the National Trust's Longcliff estate. The clear path keeps to the foot of the slopes, roughly following the line of a drystone wall on the left. It ends at Goosehill Farm where a lane, Goosehill, continues into Castleton village.

After crossing the bridge over Mill Stream turn left down a tarmac path that follows the stream's right bank. Often mallards and coots will be swimming here. The path emerges on the main street opposite the car park.

Walk 2

The Hope Valley

A circular walk exploring the pleasant pastureland and low hillslopes of the Hope Valley.
Length of walk: 5 miles.
Start/finish: Main car park, Castleton village centre.
Terrain: Easy walking on well marked paths and farm tracks.

This is one of the easiest walks in the book, and a good one to make an initial exploration of the valley, including its attractive stream, Peakhole Water. At the halfway stage it visits the neighbouring village of Hope, where you can get a cup of tea or something to eat.

Turn left out of Castleton's car park and follow the main street towards Hope. At the far end of the village a footpath signpost highlights a walled stony lane, which begins on the right hand side of the street and winds behind some cottages. Among trees to the left are the sad remains of what once must have been a substantial stone-built mill, Spital Buildings. The track ends, but the route continues as a well-defined path known as The Furlongs. It accompanies a little stream, Peakhole Water and a wire fence, passing some woodland and a small circular reservoir.

The stream veers left, leaving the path to maintain its direction across several fields. The route is well waymarked, though, with squeeze stiles in cross-walls being daubed with yellow paint. The chimney of the Hope cement works can be seen directly ahead. Two hills dominate the view. To the left is Lose Hill; to the right Win Hill. Romantics would have you believe that the names were derived from an ancient battle. The victor, King Edwin of Northumbria, was supposed to have camped out on Win Hill, while the defeated, Cuicholm of Wessex, gathered his troops on Lose Hill.

After passing the hollow of a small dyke the path temporarily becomes a little difficult to trace. Make a beeline for a prominent sign at the far edge of the field. This marks the crossing of a branch railway line used by the cement works and asks walkers to take care, and watch out for the trains. On reaching the sign, cross the railway with care and continue along the path across a field. Peakhole Water meanders towards the path again, and has

8

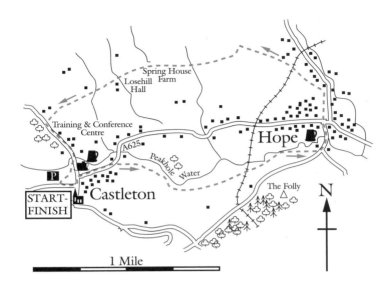

now carved a little ravine for itself. In autumn the trees that surround it are a wonderful sight. The path stays high above its banks before meeting a country lane, Pindale Road. Turn left along the lane and follow it past the church into Hope's village centre.

Turn left down the main street. Just before the Woodbine Cafe and Blacksmith's Cottage, on the right hand side of the street, a footpath signpost 'to Losehill Farm' points the way through a ginnel between houses. Go through a kissing gate and maintain direction along a street through a small housing estate. After passing Hope Clinic the route comes to a T-junction. A stile by a gate to the left of a school marks the start of a footpath across fields. It had not been signposted at the time of writing. Keep along the right edge of the first field. After going through a couple of stiles and passing some old caravans in the next field, the path veers slightly left alongside a hedge on the right. It heads towards the green pastured slopes of Lose Hill, which fill the horizon. Ignore the path to the right hereabouts as it will just take you back to the road.

A metal footbridge, hidden until the last minute, allows the crossing of the cement works branch railway line, which runs through a bramble-lined cutting. On the other side the path continues across another field towards a house. Go over the stile onto a drive, then maintain direction, passing to the right of the house, and to the left of the outbuildings beyond. Ignore the footpath signpost to the right beyond the outbuildings, but maintain direction on a path that traverses more fields with Lose Hill still directly ahead. A stile in the hedge on the right takes the route onto a narrow hedge-lined grassy track. After a short way, scale a stile on the left, beyond which the path resumes across more fields keeping the hedge to the right. It climbs to a junction of paths marked by footpath signposts.

Here, this route ignores the stile ahead, and instead turns left to follow the hedge/fence, which should be kept to the right for a while. It switches to the

opposite side of the hedge using the first stile encountered. Marker posts now highlight the route. After crossing a stream, the path is joined by a fence on the right. Ahead lie a modern house and the older cottage of Spring House Farm. Go over the stile in the fence on the right, to follow a concessionary path alongside the fence towards the farmhouse.

Beyond a gate turn left onto its drive. Once past the house, turn right along a stony lane that goes behind Losehill Hall after being joined by a lane from Field's Farm. The impressive Victorian country house was bought by The Peak Park Planning Board in 1972, and is used as a holiday and outdoor learning centre.

By now Castleton is prominent again, its grey stone cottages huddled together amid the pastures beneath Peveril Castle's ramparts. Beyond the hall at a left-hand bend in the lane, go through a stile to follow a cross-field path that soon comes to another farm track. Follow the new track past an outdoor activity centre, where a left turn along the narrow Hollowford Road brings the route back to Castleton.

Hollins Cross

A splendid circular walk climbing to the Great Ridge before visiting some of Castleton's famous showcaves.
Length of walk: 5 miles.
Start/finish: Main car park, Castleton village centre.
Terrain: A steady climb, mostly done on a narrow lane, followed by a descent on clear paths and tracks.

To the north of Castleton's huddle of cottages, the fields rise in sweeping concave slopes to a great undulating ridge. At the western end of the ridge lies Mam Tor, the Shivering Mountain: at the eastern end lies Lose Hill. To the right of Mam Tor you may spot a nick in the ridge where ancient traders and their ponies lugged their goods into Edale. Known as Hollins Cross, this nick makes a fine destination. It's a bit of a climb to get there, but it's all on well-used paths – wait until you see the views!

From the back of the car park follow the little tarmac ginnel, then turn left along Hollowford Lane, which climbs the hillsides north of the village, maintaining direction past the Hollowford Outdoor Centre. Where the lane turns sharp left and becomes an unsurfaced farm track, leave it to go through the gate straight ahead. A sunken stony path lined by hawthorn climbs the hillside to a top gate. Here a well-worn path continues in the same direction up the hillside to the high pass at Hollins Cross.

Arriving at Hollins Cross the walker sees a monument to rambler Tom Hyett surrounded by the effects of erosion, largely caused by the popularity of the Mam Tor ridge route. The memorial has a view recorder showing the positions of all the mountains on the horizon. And what a view it is!

The valley of Edale lies beneath your feet. Scattered hamlets, or booths as they are known here, lie amid a web of pastures, many framed by lines of hawthorns, which accentuate the curves of the valley. The spired church of Edale village lies tucked beneath the heather slopes of the great stony ravine of Grindsbrook. Rising above it all, the rock-fringes and rambling plateau of Kinder Scout are clothed in bracken and heather – a wonderful tweed of purple and emerald against the blue August sky.

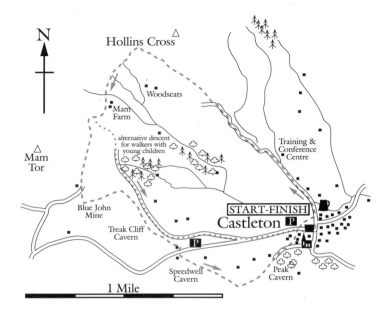

N

Hollins Cross △

Woodseats

Mam Farm

alternative descent for walkers with young children

Mam Tor △

Training & Conference Centre

Blue John Mine

START-FINISH
Castleton ℙ

Treak Cliff Cavern

ℙ

Speedwell Cavern

Peak Cavern

1 Mile

Although a popular ridge path heads for Mam Tor, today's route descends its eastern slopes (left). Beyond a stile the path weaves through some woodland that is being regenerated by the National Trust. It passes behind a couple of cottages before dropping to a stony lane just beyond them. The lane leads behind Mam Farm to reach the crumbling tarmac of the former A625 road.

Built at the turn of the 19th century to replace the old Winnats road into Castleton, this ill-conceived highway meandered down the loose shaley slopes of Mam Tor, known as the Shivering Mountain owing to its slopes' predilection for moving downhill. There were five incidences of the road shifting with the slopes, and repairs were often necessary. The inevitable happened in 1977 when serious cracks appeared in the surface. The road was closed. Gradually it has disintegrated, parts being washed down the slopes.

Here a decision has to be made, for the main route, though fairly innocuous for most walkers, includes on its descent to the Hope Valley a traverse across the steep grassy slopes beneath Treak Cliff. If it's a wet day or your children are very young and yet to attain surefootedness, it would be best to follow the old road downhill into Castleton, passing beneath the Treak Cliff Mine and Speedwell Cavern – both well worth a visit if there's time.

Those who want to continue along the main route should follow the road on its climb away from Castleton towards the Blue John Caves. Turn left down the tarmac approach road to the caves, then left again by the ticket office. Cross the stile in the fence and follow the path across fields. Beyond a stile the path narrows and descends into Castleton's wide green valley. It gradually veers right to traverse steep grassy hillslopes towards the Treak Cliff Cavern ticket office and shop. Ignore the right turn up the hillsides by the office: it's private. Treak Cliff Cavern has floodlit caves, which, although small, show off a wondrous array of stalactites.

To continue the walk turn left down the concrete steps by the ticket office before descending to the right on a concrete path with handrails. Castleton can be seen clearly further down the valley. Before reaching the road in the valley bottom, a step-stile on the right allows entry onto a narrow cross-field path that traces the course of a collapsed dry stone wall. A series of misleading sheeptracks rakes up the hillside on the right, but keep to the low path, which stays roughly parallel to the old A-road. On the approach to Speedwell Cavern the path disappears among the reeds but there are two usable stiles, one just left of the showcave ticket office and one straight ahead – both adjacent to the Winnats Road.

At the Speedwell Cavern lead miners excavated a level into the side of the hill, through which they built a subterranean canal 500 yards long. The mine didn't make much money owing to the high costs and low yields, and it soon closed. Now it's open to tourists who can take a fascinating boat trip down the canal to a landing stage just short of the Bottomless Pit, named because the spoil thrown in by miners seemingly made no impression on its depth.

On the far side of the road by the cavern building, a path takes the route through the National Trust's Longcliff estate. It skirts the slopes, and roughly follows the line of a drystone wall on the left to terminate at Goosehill Farm. Here continue along the lane, Goosehill, which heads back towards the centre of Castleton. After crossing a road bridge over Mill Stream, turn left down a tarmac path that follows the stream banks, emerging at the main street opposite the car park.

Navio Fort and Aston

**This pleasant circular walk stays on the lower verdant slopes
surrounding the River Noe, taking in a Roman fort and a high hamlet.
Length of walk: 4 miles.
Start/finish: Main car park, Hope.
Terrain: An easy walk using field paths and farm tracks, mainly in the
valley.**

Some walks more than others are meant to be taken at a leisurely pace and
combined with a good picnic. This is one of them. The picnic – well, maybe
that should be taken on the high ground above Aston where timeless views
of the fields of the Noe Valley and the surrounding peaks could be enjoyed.

From the car park turn right along the main street, then right again along
Pindale Road, which passes the church. Built largely in the 14th and 15th
centuries, this fine church with a tall spire was once at the centre of a vast
parish encompassing all of Edale and the Hope Valley, including Castleton.
In the adjacent vicarage grounds stands a 10th century Saxon cross.

Beyond the church, take the left fork, Eccles Lane, past a cottage. After a
short way, go over a stile by a gate – the place is also highlighted by a nearby
seat. The path begins as a sunken green track running roughly parallel to the
tree-lined lane at first (right), then the River Noe (below left), which has
joined its tributary, Peakhole Water, closer to the village.

The path traverses several fields, going through several gates and stiles and
passing well above a riverside campsite. In the middle stages it runs
alongside a narrow plantation of broad-leaved trees.

As the River Noe meanders through fields below and finally comes nearer,
the path dips to cross a side stream via a little footbridge. It climbs the far
banks and across a stile where it is confronted by the earthworks of Navio.
This Roman fort, built sometime around AD80, stood at a junction of roads
serving forts at Buxton, Glossop, and Templeborough. At its peak the fort
would have sheltered more than 500 soldiers. Records show that around
AD125 it was inhabited by the First Cohort of Aquitainians from South West

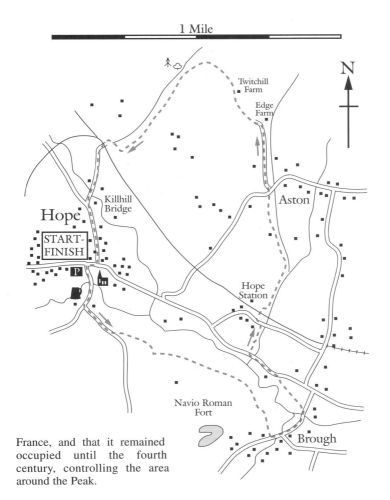

France, and that it remained occupied until the fourth century, controlling the area around the Peak.

The path straddles the earthworks to a stile in a fence at their far end. Beyond the stile it bears half right across another field to reach the B-road and Brough village. This part of the road was built along the course of the Roman Road known as Batham Gate.

Turn left along the road, passing through the village and across the footbridge over the River Noe. Beyond the bridge, go over a stile on the left next to a big gate, and aim for a big tree in the mid-distance – the path is invisible on the ground. The tree stands by the river and sets the course for a roadside stile in the hedge to the right. Once over this second stile, turn left along the A-road. The footpath is on the far side of the road.

Just beyond a charming if slightly dog-eared cottage on the right hand side of the road, a small gate marks the start of a footpath (not waymarked from here at present), which follows to the left of a hedge and dyke. It heads towards some houses and to the left of a couple of large factory warehouses. Beyond a kissing gate to the right of the houses, the path, now enclosed, swings left and climbs by some bramble thickets to a leafy tarmac lane near Hope railway station.

Turn left along the lane towards the station, then right along a narrow path that makes a beeline for the footbridge over the railway line. A right turn at the far end of the bridge brings the route to a path by a hedge. A short way along the path, turn left over a stile and cross more fields with a fence on the right. In the distance Win Hill rises above the level of the fields, its grey rocky summit tor just peeping over the verdant ridge.

Keep straight on at a crossroads of footpaths, following the signposted route 'to Win Hill'. The path curves left with the fence. Beyond the next step stile it becomes enclosed by a fence and a line of trees. After crossing a muddy patch between two stiles where a farm tractor track dissects the route, the path climbs to the road just west of the hamlet of Aston. Turn left along the road, then almost immediately right along a narrow tarmac lane, signposted 'to Win Hill'. The lane climbs past Dimings Farm to Edge Farm where you take the left fork, an unsurfaced track that climbs along the top edge of some woods.

At a footpath signpost beyond the woods, turn left downhill and through a gate on the route marked 'footpath only'. The well-defined path descends a field to another gate allowing access to Twitchill Farm. Go through the yard between the farm (right) and holiday cottages (left) and continue downhill on an unsurfaced lane, which becomes an enclosed tarmac lane halfway down. The lane turns right on meeting the Manchester to Sheffield railway line.

Turn left to go under a railway tunnel, past a railway yard, beyond which the lane doubles back left and winds its way under tree cover to the stone-built Killhill Bridge, which straddles the playful River Noe. Over the bridge, it climbs to meet the Edale road a short way north of Hope's outlying cottages. Turn left along the road, following it for half a mile/800m back to Hope.

Along the Roman Road to Hope Cross

Circular walk climbing onto the fellsides on a wide stony track once used by Roman Legionnaires. It gives wonderful views across Edale.
Length of walk: 5½ miles.
Start/finish: Main car park, Hope.
Terrain: Steady climbs on well-marked paths and farm tracks.

The path begins to the right of the Woodbine Cafe and Blacksmith's Cottage, where a footpath signpost 'to Losehill Farm' points the way through a ginnel. It threads between houses and onto a small housing estate, where the direction should be maintained past Hope Clinic to a T-junction.

Turn right along the street, past the school to the Edale road, then left along the road, passing the last of Hope's outlying cottages. After about 300yds/m, turn right along a narrow tarmac lane, signposted as a cul-de-sac, which takes the route across the River Noe at Killhill Bridge. It veers left to a railway works, then right to pass under a bridge conveying the Manchester to Sheffield railway line.

Ignore the signposted route to Win Hill, and the private road to The Homestead. Instead, continue along the lane passing to the right of the Coach House, where a gate leads into a field. Maintain your direction across the fields, keeping the field boundaries to the right all the way to Fulwood Stile Farm. Just before the farmhouse, a gate on the right leads the route onto a stony track, which in turn leads to another tarmac lane.

The lane follows the course of a Roman road linking forts at Navio near Brough, and Melandra near Glossop. Turn right along the lane, which swings left before raking up the hillsides. Ever-widening views encompass Lose Hill, which soars above the woods, fields, river and railway of the Noe valley. Beyond The Brinks, a high cottage on the right, the tree-lined lane degenerates to a rough bouldery track; still climbing, but now across fellsides of heather, sedge and bracken.

Stay with the main track: a well-used footpath takes a steeper course uphill, but offers nothing extra for the efforts that would be involved. Lose Hill has by now revealed its splendid conical shape. The sweetly pastured valley sneaks round its foot and makes a scything curve into Edale, where the darker profile of Kinder Scout moodily looks down on scattered farmhouses and cottages. The ruffled edge of sprucewoods comes into view on the right as the track achieves the ridge. The Ladybower Reservoir lies just the other side of them, but cannot be seen just yet.

Hope Cross, marked as a stone guidepost on the map, will be encountered soon after attaining the ridge. It is medieval: the 1737 refers to the date of the engraving of the surrounding parishes' initials. There was once a chapel nearby, where the ancient traveller could seek refuge and be fed, not only with the words of God but with worldly sustenance.

The old highway continues the climb to reach an intersection of tracks, where the Ladybower Reservoir comes into view beyond the spruce plantations and framed by the rocky tors on Crook Hill. At the intersection the Roman soldiers would have gone straight on, heading for the Woodlands Valley. Our route, however, turns left beyond the stile, descending along the

N

Hope Cross
Guide Post
Ladybower Reservoir
Jaggers Clough
Roman Road
Edale End
Upper Fulwood Farm
Wooler Knoll
Hope Brink
Oaker Farm
Fulwood Stile Farm
Town Head Bridge
Killhill Bridge
START-FINISH
Hope
1 Mile

wide path signposted to Edale, which now stretches out beyond the deep wooded chasm of Jaggers Clough.

After going through a metal five-bar gate, turn left along a grooved track (not signposted or waymarked) that descends gradually downhill and alongside a wire fence. Beyond a stile the well-defined grassy track forges through bracken, high above and parallel to Jaggers Clough. The chimney of Hope cement works should be seen straight ahead in the distance.

The track meets a concessionary path that has descended Jaggers Clough just before reaching Upper Fulwood Farm, which is run by the National Trust. Turn right through a gate into the farmyard, then left in front of the house, following a metalled lane past the information barn.

Leave the lane beyond the bridge over the River Noe to follow a path on the right climbing steep grassy banks to the Edale Road. Across the road, follow the unsurfaced lane that tucks under the railway bridge and climbs through woodland above Fiddle Clough. At its end in the pleasant woodland, a path on the left begins with some concrete steps up to a stile. It continues across fields, staying close to the fence on the left. Do not be tempted onto a prominent farm track cutting across the route, for it heads back to the road. At this point the fence veers left away from the track, but it soon rejoins the route. The path passes to the right of Oaker Farm, where it is tightly confined by barbed wire for a short distance. After rain, it can be slippery hereabouts.

Beyond the farm, descend to join a stony lane that passes the impressive Moorgate and Oakleigh B&Bs before declining to the Edale road. Turn right along the road. After about a quarter of a mile, turn right on a signposted path: the spot is highlighted by a post box in the wall. The path follows the field edge to farm outbuildings.

Once over the stile by the buildings turn left on a track, passing to the left of a cottage. Go over the stile straight ahead and follow the path across the bridge over the railway cutting. Follow the path across the fields towards Hope, passing a couple of caravans and coming to the road by the school. Go straight ahead into a small housing estate and follow the ginnel on the left back into Hope's village centre.

Win Hill

Win Hill is one of the finest places in the Peak District. Choose a fine, settled day and your efforts will be rewarded by superb views.
Length of walk: 5¹/₂ miles.
Start/finish: Main car park, Hope.
Terrain: A mixture of farm tracks, field paths and a well-defined route through heather moor to the rocky summit crest.

Compared with many of the others in this book, this is a fairly strenuous walk and includes a moderate climb to Win Hill's summit. Even in summer you need either good boots or trainers with a good grip. If there is the slightest chance of rain take a waterproof, for it can get cold on the tops.

From the car park turn right along the main road through Hope. Turn left along the lane signposted to Edale. After about 600yds/m, beyond the last of the village's houses, take the narrow tarmac lane on the right, signposted as a cul-de-sac. It descends to cross the River Noe at Killhill Bridge before veering left to pass a railway works. After going under the railway bridge turn right on a lane signposted 'to Win Hill'.

The lane follows the course of the railway at first then swings left uphill to Twitchill Farm. Continue between the farmhouse (left) and some holiday cottages (right) to a gate through which a clear path climbs the steep, grassy hillslopes to another gate where there is a signposted crossroads of routes.

A direct and steep route to Win Hill's summit lies straight ahead. However, an easier but longer route that can be used on this occasion turns left along the bridleway running beneath the conifers of Top Plantation. It rakes across the hillslopes before meeting the ridge route on Wooler Knoll, where vast plantations of spruce, larch and pine cloak the north-eastern slopes.

Turn right here and follow the path along the spine of the whaleback ridge.

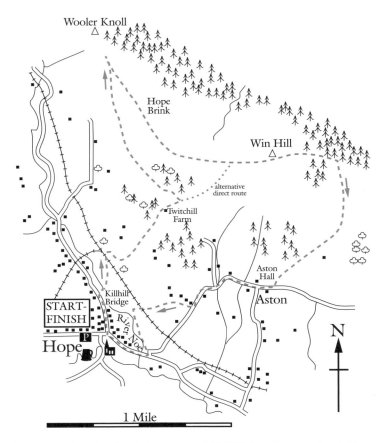

A concrete trig point shows the true top, 1,516ft/462m above sea level. From it the walker can see one of the Peak's finest views. There's a tale to tell about the naming of Win Hill and Lose Hill. It concerns two warlords, Edwin, the first Christian king of Northumbria, and Cuicholm, King of Wessex, who engaged in a fierce battle on the slopes of the Hope Valley. Apparently Cuicholm murdered his enemy's maidservant Lilla. Edwin, who was victorious and had his revenge, camped here on Win Hill, while Cuicholm camped on Lose Hill, hence the names.

Maintain the direction of ascent on descending the summit rocks to a stile in a fence where a wide track continues through heather and sparse pine down to dense conifers of the Win Hill Plantation.Turn at a crossroads of tracks at the edge of the forest proper. The splendid sunken track along the brow of the hill is surrounded by heather, gorse and bilberry. It affords fascinating views across the Derwent Valley to Bamford Moor, whose steep sides are cloaked with bracken and capped with gritstone bluffs. Further afield the rock fringed edges of Stanage and Froggatt fade into the blue mist of the horizon.

Keep a watch for the beginning of the path down to Aston. It begins just beyond a stone cattle drinking trough and climbs half right to a gap in the wall. The clear path continues through rough hillslopes before descending to meet a wide grassy track by a tall drystone wall. Climb some steps in the wall before resuming the descent across more cultivated pastures. A hedge by a dyke sets the direction to the bottom right hand corner of the field, where a step stile allows entry to a very narrow pasture – keep on the left hand side of this, ignoring a prominent track to the right halfway down. Beyond another step stile the path becomes confined by bramble, fern and a few nettles. Follow it to the narrow tarmac lane at Aston.

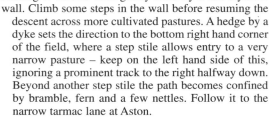

Turn right along the lane, passing through the handful of pretty stone-built cottages, including the 16th century Aston Hall. The lane winds down the hill. Ignore the first two lanes on the right: the first signposted to Win Hill: the second to Birchfield Hall. A hundred yards or so beyond a sharp left hand bend, take the third on the right, passing a listed Caravan Club site. Take the left fork by the farmhouse. A hundred yards further, go through a small gate (there is no footpath signpost at the time of writing) and descend to the bottom right-hand corner of the field (no path on the ground).

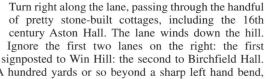

Here go over a step stile into the shade of some trees, and follow the twisting path under the railway tunnel. Over another stile at the far end, turn right, then follow the hedge on the right down to the River Noe. Turn left here ignoring the kissing gate (R), and follow the riverbank to the A625 road bridge, just east of Hope. Climb the bridge's steps, then turn right along the road back to the village.

The Derwent Reservoirs

A pleasant Derwent Valley walk taking in the contrasting landscapes of wild moor, forest and lake.
Length of walk: 6 miles.
Start: Kings Tree, reached by bus from the Fairholmes car park beneath the Derwent Reservoir dam.
Finish: Fairholmes car park.
Terrain: An easy walk on stony tracks round the reservoir shores.

A circuit of the Upper Derwent valley and its reservoirs makes one of the finest low routes in the Peak, but for many it is too long and involves some road walking. However, by taking the bus from the Fairholmes car park up the west side of the valley to Kings Tree, the road walking can be eliminated and the length of the walk reduced to manageable proportions.

From the little roundabout by the bus stop at the end of the tarmac road, go through the gate and follow the flinted forest road that continues between the spruce trees and the Howden Reservoir. It descends to a splendid but isolated twin arched bridge at Slippery Stones. This 17th-century bridge once spanned the river further south at Derwent village, but the construction of the Ladybower dam, which began in 1935, meant that the whole area would be submerged beneath the waters of the Derwent. The bridge was dismantled and the stones numbered. In 1959, it was reconstructed.

Cross the bridge and turn left on a path that meets a stony track that has traced the eastern shores of Howden Reservoir. Turn left along the track, which traverses a wide, grassy area at the foot of Cranberry Clough. At a ford, cross the stream on a footbridge to the left, before continuing with the track along the east side of the river. The sprucewoods have now been left behind and the walk enters the Upper Derwent valley. Scattered oaks surround the river, and the hills close in to form a narrow ravine.

The valley swings left beyond Broadhead Clough and the track follows suit on its way to the inner recesses of Bleaklow. Although the view is a spectacular one with rocky escarpments of Crow Stones and Horse Stone Naze crowding the fast flowing River Derwent, it's time to turn back to

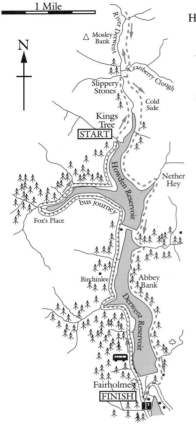

discover the eastern shores of the Howden and Derwent Reservoirs.

Retrace the outward route down the valley to Slippery Stones, but stay with the stony track rather than descending to the bridge. It climbs above a thin strip of woodland and at the foot of the steep flanks of Cold Side, where the river widens to become the Howden Reservoir. The track rounds the sides of Cow Hey, looping into Howden Clough before resuming its southerly course down the main valley to the stone-built Howden Dam.

The Howden Reservoir was the first of the Derwent Reservoirs to be started in 1901: the Derwent was started a year later. To facilitate the moving of stone from Longshaw Quarry near Bamford, the Derwent Water Board built a railway that terminated just short of the site of the Howden Dam. Workers were housed in a temporary village of corrugated iron huts. Tin Town, as it was known, was sited at the foot of Birchinlee Pasture on the far side of the Derwent Reservoir. By 1917 the project was finished. The two hundred-foot-plus high dams held back 4,100 million gallons of water, which submerged beautiful pastures.

The track continues alongside the eastern shores of the Derwent Reservoir, passing beneath more conifers and rhododendron bushes. Nearly two miles later it reaches the Derwent Dam, where there is a memorial to 617 Squadron – the Dambusters, who buzzed this place on low-level practices for their May 1943 raid on the Moehne and Eder Dams in Germany. At the side of the dam, take the little path on the right, descending through the woods down to a tarmac lane at its foot. Turn right along the lane, which leads back to the Fairholmes car park, where there's a shop.

The Derwent Edge and Ladybower Reservoir

A superb walk to gritstone tors with views across Derwent Reservoirs.
Length of walk: 5 miles.
Start/finish: Car park/lay-by on Snake Road just west of Ladybower.
Terrain: A moderate climb to the ridge followed by well-defined bridleway and an unsurfaced lane by the Ladybower Reservoir.

From the car park follow the road across the Ladybower viaduct. Just beyond the reservoir crossing turn left on a metalled private road that zigzags past a few of Ashopston's remaining cottages – many were sunk when the valley was flooded beneath Ladybower Reservoir in 1946.

Where the road ends in a walled area, go through the gate on the left and double back up the hillside on a forestry track climbing through pines and larches. The track, which can be muddy in winter, leaves the forest and continues its steady climb beneath the precipitous sides of Lead Hill. Ladybower Reservoir comes into view far below, twisting through green pastures and dark sprucewoods. Wild moorland ridges top this cultivated landscape, stretching to the Bleaklow massif that sprawls across the skyline.

The zigzag path to the ridge shown on the OS map has long been replaced by a well-worn direct climb to the ridge. Here leave the bridleway to climb left to the rocks of Whinstone Lee Tor. Splendid gritstone rocks cap the fine summit. Views make the effort well worthwhile. The angular summit profile of Kinder Scout peeps over Crook Hill's craggy crests, and glares darkly across Edale at the greener Mam Tor ridge, while to the south, the gritstone cliffs of Stanage and Bamford Edge fringe their heather-clad escarpments.

The continuing path follows the ridge past the Hurkling Stones. Ahead, a series of rocky tors caps the ridge, notably the block-like Coach and Horses in the mid-distance and the angular summit rocks on Dovestone Tor. Beyond the Hurkling Stones, in a slight dip in the ridge, the route meets a clear signposted path linking Ladybower Reservoir and Moscar. Turn left along this and follow it down the hillside towards the reservoir. Turn right to follow a wallside path that joins from the left. After a short way the new path

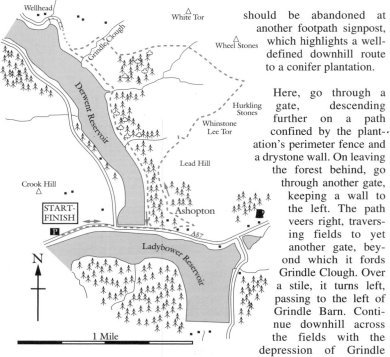

should be abandoned at another footpath signpost, which highlights a well-defined downhill route to a conifer plantation.

Here, go through a gate, descending further on a path confined by the plantation's perimeter fence and a drystone wall. On leaving the forest behind, go through another gate, keeping a wall to the left. The path veers right, traversing fields to yet another gate, beyond which it fords Grindle Clough. Over a stile, it turns left, passing to the left of Grindle Barn. Continue downhill across the fields with the depression of Grindle Clough on the left, before swinging right to a stile, across which lies an unsurfaced lane tracing the eastern shores of Ladybower Reservoir.

The way back to the car is left, but, if the Ladybower's waters are low, it would be worth detouring right along the unsurfaced lane to the bridge over Mill Beck. At such times the crumbled walls and foundations of Derwent village would surface. A notice board pinpoints the positions of Derwent Hall, the old post office, school, church and some of the old cottages.

Retrace your steps down the lane and continue southwards along the shores of the reservoir. After rounding Grainfoot Clough the lane passes beneath woodlands with the rocks of Whinstone Lee Tor crowning the hilltop. Finally beyond a wide gate, it meets the outward route above the Ashopton viaduct. Descend to the main road and follow it right, continuing over the viaduct and back to the car park.

Stanage Edge

Perhaps this is the book's most spectacular high route, taking walkers along a lofty ridge where climbers tackle the vertical gritstone cliffs. Length of walk: 6 miles. Start/finish: Car park beneath Stanage Plantation high on the hillside two miles north of Hathersage. Terrain: An easy walk along firm footpaths, mainly alongside cliffs.

The gritstone cliffs of Stanage Edge fringe the skyline above Hathersage, often gleaming gold above biscuit-coloured grasses and purple heather. High roads from the village make easy walks possible above and below the three miles of crags. Follow the well-used path from the back of the car park towards the imposing cliffs. The path is joined by one from the right and soon enters the mixed woodland of Stanage Plantation via a gate. Now paved with weather-beaten millstone grit slabs, the path weaves through the woods to a top gate. Go through the gate and climb the paved path known as Jacob's Ladder. The ingenious route, which is believed to be of Roman origin, rakes across heathered slopes to find a gap in the rocks through which to climb to the top of the cliffs. Looking back, half of Derbyshire is beneath your feet. The soft green fields of the Derwent and Hope valleys are framed by the green hills of limestone country in the south, the shapely Mam Tor Ridge and the darker heather-clad gritstone moors of Kinder and Bleaklow to the north.

Turn left and follow the path along the cliff edge until you meet a wide bouldery track coming up from the left. Descend along it for a short way before leaving it for a path that follows the lower edge of the cliffs. In rough enclosures below lies a gigantic boulder, known as the Buck Stone. It was once a shelter for the packhorse men or jaggers who would halt here for refreshment and to rest the ponies before tackling the summit. This new path gives a fine view of the crags and cliffs of Stanage: you may see climbers pitting their skills against the perpendicular rocks. Don't impede them. Nineteenth century pioneers such as J W Putrell founded several gully routes. In the 1950s the talented Joe Brown and Don Whillans forged even harder climbs. As the sport became more popular the number of routes grew until Stanage had well over 500 climbs.

The hard gritstone that forms the rocks was used for making millstones, hence its name, Millstone Grit. The importance of Sheffield as a steel-making centre grew as a result of its proximity to this plentiful supply. The millstones were cut on the quarry sites high on the hill and you will see some lying around. There were two types. The modern and larger ones were wheel shaped with a small hole through the centre, while the older type were convex on one side, rather like a mushroom. The industry declined in the mid-19th century with the import of superior millstones from France. This caused a riot in the mills where militants smashed the foreign stones. The industry died not long afterwards with the introduction of roller mills.

The little path rounds the protruding crags of Crow Chin, so named because a quarry worker looked up and thought he saw a giant crow coming down from the skies. He must have had some imagination! By now the moorland below has risen to a marshy saddle between Moscar and Bamford Moors, and wilderness prevails. The A57 highway climbs through a gap in the dark Pennine hills of the Derwent Edge. With each footstep the cliff edge becomes less defined and the cliffs gradually become splintered until they are little more than rashes of boulders. But the crags of Stanage End stand out as the last bastion overlooking the sombre, rushy moors.

Just beyond Stanage End the ridge path comes in from the right. Double back on this path and stride out along the top edge. Heather takes root again and soon you are standing on the rocks of Crow Chin, which still doesn't look the part no matter how one stares at it. Numbered rock basins now line the route along the top. The numbers were neatly sculpted by gamekeepers at the turn of the century. Their purpose was to keep a plentiful supply of water for the grouse.

Continue to the concrete trig point that caps High Neb, which at 458m/1,502ft is the highest point reached on the whole walk. Further along the edge, the broad, bouldery track descended earlier in the walk comes in from the right. This time stay on the cliff edge until there's a fork in the tracks. Take the left one, a wide, partially paved track known as the Long Causeway, which traverses the heather moor to Stanage Pole.

The track is said to be of Roman origin, probably built under the governorship of Agricola. More recently it would have been used by the packhorse men and for the transport of millstones to Sheffield. The pole would have been a landmark for these travellers. Views from it encompass the wide plains of southern Yorkshire. Now leave the old highway and double back along a grassy groove through the heather of White Path Moss, back to the gritstone edge. Turn left along the edge and watch out for Robin

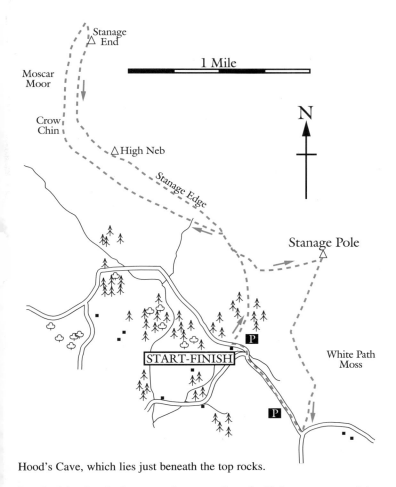

Hood's Cave, which lies just beneath the top rocks.

Locals claim that the famous outlaw came from the Hathersage area and that he hid from the Sheriff of Nottingham many times in the cave. They also claim that his trusty sidekick, Little John, lies buried under a yew tree in Hathersage churchyard. Several hundred yards/m beyond the cave a path on the right takes the route away from the edge and downhill to a road close to a T-junction. Turn right along the road, passing a car park. Take the right fork at the next junction to return to the car.

Carl Wark and Burbage Rocks

Circular walk over craggy heather-clad escarpments offering fine lofty views of the Derwent Valley.
Length of walk: 5 miles.
Start/finish: Longshaw NT car park by Fox House Inn, just off the A625 between Hathersage and Sheffield.
Terrain: Fairly easy walk on a stony track and moorland paths.

In 1927 the Duke of Rutland put his Longshaw Estate up for sale. It had been considered a fine grouse moor but also included the lodge and its carefully planned grounds and woodland. A charity was set up and the land donated to the National Trust who kept it open for the public. This walk takes full advantage of the freedom of the estate and climbs from the lodge to the heights.

Take the narrow path from the back of the car park heading away from the hillside towards the Longshaw lodge. The main lodge, an impressive gothic building of darkened millstone grit, has now been turned into apartments, but the adjacent building has been set up as a cafe and visitor centre. Turn right at the junction with an unsurfaced lane, following the signs to the Longshaw Visitor Centre.

Turn right at the visitor centre, following the drive to the B-road. On the opposite side of the road, staggered to the left, a signpost shows a well-defined footpath through woodland. In spring the woodland carpets are splashed with the purple of the common dog violet, the yellow of lesser celandine, and the delicate pinks of wood sorrel.

Take the right fork in the paths. It leads to the A-road immediately opposite a stony cart track known as the Duke of Rutland's Drive. This old highway takes the walk into an amphitheatre of heather and gritstone. On the right side are the cliffs of the Burbage Rocks, on the left, the impressive craggy knolls of Carl Wark and Higger Tor.

Duke's Drive chooses a low route beneath Burbage Rocks. It may sound unexciting but it retains the feeling of walking through this great arena with Carl Wark towering into the sky. After a short while a little packhorse bridge comes into view. Shaded by the conifers that bask around Burbage Brook, the surroundings look ideal for a picnic. The route will pass the bridge on the return route. For now, though, it aims for higher things and continues along the stony track beneath the Burbage Rocks, where climbers grapple with the solid gritstone buttresses that fringe the heathered slopes.

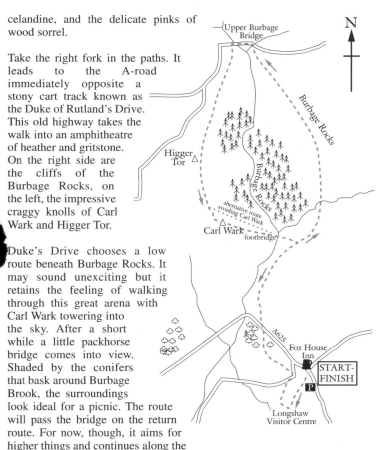

The path terminates at a stile by Ringinglow Road high on the hillside, just east of Upper Burbage Bridge. Turn left along the road for a short way to the high car park, which is usually frequented by a snack sales van. It's a popular spot for motorists, who come for a cup of tea or an ice cream with a view. The next objective, Higger Tor, or Higher Tor, juts out from the skies, interrupting the view down to the Derwent Valley. A stile gives access for a return to the moors. Beyond it there are two paths. The higher right fork is best, choosing to head more directly across the heather towards Higger Tor. After dipping slightly at Fiddler's Elbow it climbs on an eroded course to the top of this shapely gritstone hill.

The splendid little summit has enough rocks and bouldered perches to seat the masses, and plenty of nature's own sculptures to inspire a budding Henry Moore. Carl Wark appears as a squat boulder-strewn knoll from hereabouts, rising from the bracken and heather. The path from the south end of the summit scrambles between rocks and continues across bracken and tussocky moor before the easy climb to Carl Wark. For those who do not find the idea of another peak appealing, take the left fork in the paths just short of Carl Wark's rocky ramparts. It descends into the combe and to the right of sprucewoods, where it comes upon the packhorse bridge across Burbage Brook.

Those who want to go to the summit just climb a wide path between the rocks. It's steep but short. The summit is a former fort, which historians once believed to be of Iron Age origins. They now think it dates back to around the 7th century. The hill's natural fortifications were enhanced by the laying of huge rocks, creating a 10ft/3m rampart along the only weakness. Weird-shaped weathered rocks scattered all over the top offer protection from the elements and perches on which to enjoy a well-earned drink or snack.

The path descends from rocks to the left and just short of the plateau's south-western tip. After scrambling down the rocks it weaves through bracken, heather and moor grass to the bottom end of the spruce plantations. Here the high and low routes meet and descend to the previously mentioned packhorse bridge.

Cross the bridge over Burbage Brook and go straight ahead on a path across rough moorland to climb back to the Duke of Rutland's drive. Turn right along the drive, retracing the outward route back to the road. Across the road take the path into the woodlands of the Longshaw Estate and turn left, back to the B-road across which lies the footpath to the lodge and the car park.